How To
Make Your
Own Movies

How To Make Your Own Movies

an introduction to filmmaking

by
Harvey Weiss

Young Scott Books

A Young Scott Book
Addison-Wesley Publishing Company
Reading, Massachusetts 01867
Printed in the United States of America

Library of Congress Cataloging in Publication Data

Weiss, Harvey.
How to make your own movies.
SUMMARY: Discusses planning, preparation, and
basic techniques for making a film.
1. Cinematography—Juvenile literature.
[1. Cinematography.   2. Amateur motion pictures]
I. Title.
TR851.W44   778.5'3   72-11650
ISBN 0-201-09310-3

DEFGHIJKLM-WZ-8987654321

CONTENTS

A note about the illustrations: 8mm or Super 8 movie film is clear and sharp when projected on a movie screen. However, an individual frame, when it is enlarged and reproduced in a book, is usually unsatisfactory. For this reason most of the photographs in this book were made with a 35mm still camera. In many cases where an actual movie is described, the action was photographed with the still camera as well as with the movie camera, so that good, clear pictures would be available to use in the book.

Thanks and acknowledgments are due the following individuals and organizations who generously assisted the author in many ways: Robert Baxter, Bernard Burroughs, Seth Cushman, Margaret Morris, Matthew Morris, Jonathan and Jay Satz, Carla Stevens, Sanford Weiss, Elizabeth Weiss, John Weiss, The Arriflex Company of America, Bauer Cameras, Bell and Howell, Bolex/Paillard, Cannon Cameras, Eastman Kodak Company, Nikon Company, Vivitar Cameras.

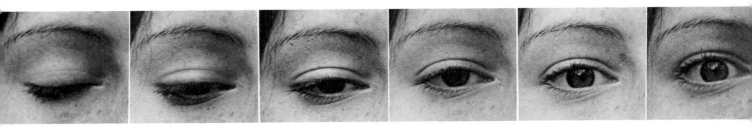

Introduction

Movies are a part of our lives. You see them all the time; in the theatre, in schools, on television. Everything shown on television — from a fifteen-second commercial to a full-length feature — is some kind of a movie. So it is only natural that most people will think at one time or another, "Wouldn't it be fun to make a movie?"

Yes, it would be. It is *enormous* fun!

And it isn't difficult. Modern cameras are simple and foolproof. The film is just popped into the camera without any fussing around. The exposure is completely automatic. Just about all you do is focus and press the trigger. If you are using an older, hand-me-down camera, there may be some additional, more complicated operations, but this is all explained in the first chapter of this book.

Most people who own a camera use it in a very ordinary, "snapshooting" kind of way. They take movies of family visits, or a child learning to ride a bicycle, or scenes of the Grand Canyon, or a birthday party in the backyard. Movies like these are fine. Everybody enjoys them. Everybody loves to see themselves on the screen. But after a few films of this sort, when the novelty of a new camera has worn off, the question will be asked, "What now?"

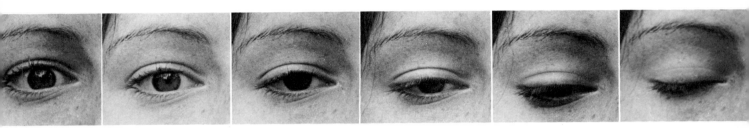

This book tries to answer that question because there is a great deal you can do. There are exciting, creative, provocative things that can be done with a movie camera. And with a little experience it is possible to make entertaining and imaginative films about even the most ordinary events.

The amateur filmmaker can work in many different ways, depending on his interests and experience. There are filmmakers who like to write their own stories and use their friends or relatives as actors. Some people like to make nature films, or sport films, or abstract films using only shapes and colors, or films that have a tape-recorded sound track. Animated films are surprisingly easy to make. Many filmmakers are concerned with problems of ecology, housing, poverty, or politics, and make movies that have something to say about these problems. It is possible to make dramatic and interesting movies based on common, everyday events. If you have a little bit of imagination, and acquire some of the know-how explained on these pages, you may even be able to make a simply great, spine-tingling, super-colossal, four-star, epic film about something as simple as someone learning to ride a bicycle!

The point is that filmmaking can be more than just an amusing, but unplanned, record of miscellaneous events. It can be a creative, meaningful, and very exciting art form.

Nikon

1. The Equipment

The most essential piece of equipment is, of course, the camera. There are three basic types to choose from. One camera uses 8mm film. (The *mm* stands for millimeter; 8mm film is 8 millimeters wide.) Another type of camera uses 16mm film.

The third type uses Super 8 film, and this is the most common movie camera used by most amateurs. Super 8 film is actually the same width as 8mm film, but the sprocket holes are smaller. This allows more room for the photographic image, and thus the projected picture is larger and sharper.

There are also larger cameras and larger film sizes, but they are only used for commercial or Hollywood-type productions.

The Super 8 Camera

This is the most popular type of camera used today. Unless you are taking pictures under very odd and unusual conditions, or unless you make some gross error, you can be sure of getting technically excellent results. The modern Super 8 camera is a marvel of miniature electrical engineering. It contains one or more tiny electric motors, and can make all sorts of automatic adjustments that in older cameras have to be performed by the cameraman. These cameras are powered by batteries that will usually last for a great many rolls of film.

8

Bolex

Vivitar

Eastman Kodak

Eastman Kodak

Eastman Kodak

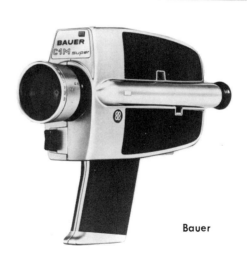

Bauer

These are all Super 8 movie cameras. As you can see they seem pretty much alike. But their quality and special features vary a great deal. The prices also vary greatly. The very simplest camera costs less than forty dollars. The more elaborate camera with a high quality zoom lens and many adjustments will cost several times that amount.

THE FILM   Super 8 film comes in a cartridge. To load the film, you simply open up the camera and slip the cartridge into the proper place. Close the camera and you are all set to go. When you've exposed the film, remove the cartridge and have it processed. There is no danger of putting a used roll of film back into your camera, because the word "exposed" is written on the end of the film.

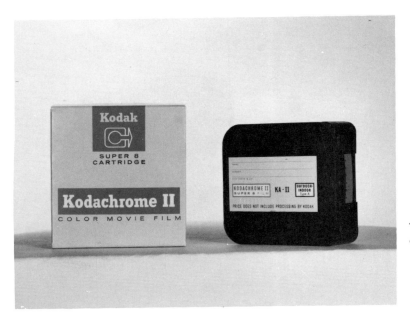

This is what a Super 8 cartridge and the box containing it looks like.

FOCUSING   In most Super 8 cameras, the lens which directs the image onto the film is also used for focusing. What you see in the viewfinder is what the film sees. This is particularly useful when you are taking close-ups.

You focus the camera lens by rotating it. You can see when the image is sharpest. If your camera has a separate viewfinder, you will have to estimate how far you are from your subject. Then you focus by rotating the lens. Various distances are marked along the side of the lens, and you simply turn until the proper distance is indicated.

EXPOSURE   Most Super 8 cameras have an automatic exposure control. This is an amazing device which has been used on cameras only for the last few years. It automatically sets the lens opening for the lighting conditions in the scene at which you are pointing the camera. The diagram below shows how it works. The electric eye senses the brightness or dimness of the scene and then directs a tiny motor either to open up or

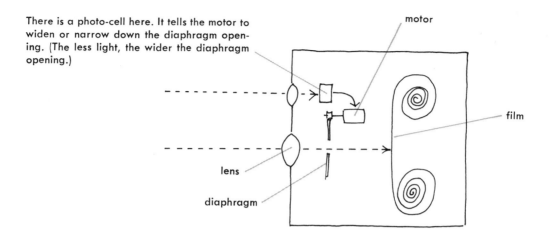

There is a photo-cell here. It tells the motor to widen or narrow down the diaphragm opening. (The less light, the wider the diaphragm opening.)

motor

film

lens

diaphragm

close down the diaphragm behind the lens. On very bright, sunny days or well-lit subjects, the electric eye will decrease the size of the diaphragm opening. When the camera is pointing at a dim or poorly lit scene, the electric eye will cause the diaphragm to open up, allowing more light to reach the film.

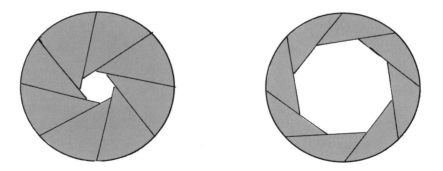

However, this exposure-control mechanism is not infallible. The electric eye reads the overall scene. If, for example, you are photographing someone's head against a background of very dark trees, the electric eye will be influenced by the dark background. It will read the trees as well as the head, and the diaphragm setting will probably be wrong for the head. Too much light will reach the film, and the face will be overexposed.

Here is an instance where the large area of shadow in the background will cause the automatic exposure control to set the camera for a subject in shadow.

Here the very light background will affect the exposure control so that the diaphragm will be set for a subject in bright light, though actually the face is in shadow.

A similiar error can occur (in the opposite way) if a dark subject is placed in front of a brilliant white background. To prevent this kind of error, bring the camera up quite close to the subject, so that the electric eye will not include much of the background.

On some of the better Super 8 cameras, there is a brightness control. It is marked "backlight" or "spotlight." You would use the setting for "backlight" if you were shooting a subject with a great deal of light behind it. You'd use the "spotlight" setting if the subject was well lit and the background was much darker.

With cameras that have an automatic exposure control there is also some kind of warning signal that shows when there is too much or too little light for a proper exposure.

If you have a Super 8 camera that does not have an automatic exposure control, you will have to follow the procedure used with the regular 8mm cameras, as explained on page 16. If you are shooting indoors with artificial light, see page 65.

THE ZOOM LENS   This is one more remarkable feature that most Super 8 cameras have. It is a special lens which can be a wide-angle lens, a normal lens, or a telephoto lens.

The wide-angle lens is usually used when there is a large area you want to include in the picture. If, for example, you were in a small room and there was a lot of action you wanted to

This is the effect you can get with a zoom lens. You start with a general view of the situation and gradually close in, ending with a close-up of the most significant or dramatic part of the action. In this case, it is the brush and can of paint. It is also possible to start with the close-up and zoom away to the larger, overall view.

capture, you would probably choose a wide-angle setting that would include as much of the scene as possible.

If you were far away from something and wanted to get it on film as large as possible, you would use the telephoto setting. This kind of lens acts like a telescope.

Some zoom lenses are worked by a little electric motor. You press a button and the lens changes from one type to another. Press another button and it changes back. Other zoom lenses have a little handle which you shift in order to change.

You have no doubt seen movies or sports films where the camera will suddenly move in on the subject, increasing it in size in a very startling way. This is a zoom shot, and most beginners can't resist this very dramatic effect. But it quickly gets tiresome if overdone. It is much better to set the lens for the kind of angle and magnification you want, and then leave it that way for the duration of the scene. Zoom in or out only when there is a good reason to do so.

A point to bear in mind when using the telephoto setting of a zoom lens is that the focus is more critical. This presents a slight problem if you are going to zoom from wide angle to telephoto

Shots like these would be almost impossible without a telephoto lens or the zoom lens set at telephoto. A telephoto lens enables you to take close-ups without actually getting too near your subject, or being eaten up.

while the camera is running. There is a good possibility that what seemed in focus at wide-angle will become out of focus at telephoto, because this latter setting is so much more critical. What you should do is first focus at the telephoto setting, then set the lens at wide-angle, start the camera and proceed with your shot. The focus will be sharp at all times. If the lens is properly focused at the telephoto setting, it will be in focus for the entire zoom range.

Most movie cameras also have an adjustment for slow motion or fast motion. This is very useful and is explained on page 84.

The 8mm Camera

This type of camera is being gradually replaced by the newer, Super 8 cameras. However, if you are given a hand-me-down camera, or are borrowing somebody else's camera, it may turn out to be this kind. If you have limited funds and are going to buy a secondhand camera, you will be able to get an 8mm camera (as well as the projector) very much cheaper than the more popular Super 8. The cost of film is about the same for both cameras.

This is what a roll of regular 8mm film looks like.

LOADING THE FILM   8mm film comes in a roll. Open the side of the camera, insert the spool so that the light-colored side of the film (the emulsion side) is facing the lens. This should be done in a subdued light. Then thread the film through the proper channels and onto the take-up spool. Before you close the camera, run off a few frames of the film, observing carefully that everything is working smoothly and that the film is being wound up on the take-up spool. Then close the cover, run off about two feet, and you're ready to go. That first two feet of film is removed at the processing laboratory, so you aren't being wasteful.

When the entire roll is run through the camera it will be wound up on the take-up spool. Now remove this spool, flip it over and place it where the original roll of film was. Then repeat the same steps as when you first loaded the film, and you are ready to take more movies. What you are doing is running the one roll of film through the camera twice.

You can do this because 8mm film is only 8mm film *after* it has been processed. The processing laboratory develops the film, splits it in half, and then splices the two halves together. When you load your camera you are actually loading with 16mm film. The first time it is run through the camera, half the film is exposed. Then, when it is run through the second time, the other half is exposed.

EXPOSURE   With most 8mm cameras you must set the exposure yourself. This is done by rotating a little ring which is a part of the lens mounting. When you rotate this ring, you are either widening or narrowing the diaphragm of the lens, as explained on page 11. The wider the opening, the more light will pass through the lens. The smaller the opening the less light. If you look into the lens you will be able to see the diaphragm open or close as the ring is turned. On bright, sunny days you need less light for a proper exposure. On cloudy, dark days you need more light.

The various openings of the diaphragm are given f/ numbers which will probably read like this; f/2, f/2.8, f/4, f/5.6, f/8, f/11, f/16. The smaller the number, the *wider* the opening. A setting of f/2 allows more light to reach the film than a setting of f/4.

But what is the right setting for any given light condition? You can get this information from the slip of paper that comes with your film. If, for example, you are using Kodachrome II you will find that the recommended exposure for a subject in bright sunlight would be f/8. On a cloudy day with your subject in the shade, the recommended exposure would be f/2.8, and so on.

FOCUSING   With many of the older 8mm cameras you cannot look through the viewfinder and adjust the lens until the image is sharpest. Some of the more inexpensive cameras have a fixed-focus lens. This means that everything from about five feet to infinity is in focus, and there is no adjustment that you can make. ("Infinity" as used by photographers refers to any distance more than a hundred feet or so. It is indicated by this mark: ∞) Other cameras will have a series of numbers engraved on the side of the lens. These refer to the distance from lens to subject, and you will have to measure or guess how far away your subject is. Then you rotate the lens until this distance is opposite an arrow or dot. Now the lens is set for that particular distance and everything that far from the camera will be in sharp focus.

Most of the older 8mm cameras do not have the sort of zoom lens described on page 12. But you can still get telephoto or wide-angle shots by buying these two extra lenses. Then you simply unscrew the normal lens and replace it with one of these others. Some cameras have a "turret." Three different lenses are mounted on a rotating metal plate. You turn the plate to change from one lens to another.

There is another type of 8mm camera which uses film that comes in a magazine, or slim metal case. (Don't confuse this with Super 8 cartridges.) This type of camera isn't quite as common as the others mentioned here. If you happen to get your hands on one, you'll find that the instruction slip that comes with the film will provide all the know-how needed.

The 16mm Camera

This kind of camera is considerably larger and bulkier than either 8mm or Super 8 cameras. Because the film is a large size, the image projected on the screen is larger and sharper than with the smaller cameras. For this reason a 16mm camera is often used in making films for TV, for schools, and even for projection in some movie theatres.

Most 16mm cameras are complex and have a variety of lenses, or one zoom lens. They usually have many adjustments so that different kinds of special effects are possible. But this is not a camera for the beginner—if only because of the expenses involved.

Arriflex

Bolex

Bolex

Here are some 16mm cameras. They are quite elaborate, beautifully constructed pieces of equipment, not what a beginner would be likely to use. But some day when you become an expert, or perhaps a professional filmmaker you might use cameras like these. The camera on the left, which is electrically powered, has a large zoom lens and an over-size magazine that holds a 400-foot reel of film. This camera permits uninterrupted filming for over eleven minutes.

Film and processing for 16mm cameras is very much more expensive than for 8mm or Super 8. When a five-minute roll of 16mm film, with processing, costs something like fourteen dollars, most amateur filmmakers will think twice (and probably reject) any notion for a somewhat ambitious movie that might require a half-dozen rolls of film. The camera itself, as well as projector, editing equipment, and other odds and ends, can run into many hundreds of dollars.

There are a great many different kinds of cameras available today. It is impossible to describe them all. Most of the newer Super 8 cameras are similiar, but once you start looking at older cameras, the variations and unfamiliar adjustments may seem confusing. If you are using someone else's camera make sure everything about it is very carefully explained to you before you take it. If you buy a secondhand camera, take somebody along who knows something about cameras, and make sure that the salesman explains everything to you in complete detail. If you have a new camera, read the instruction manual that comes with it. Then read it again, and then a few more times, so that you understand very clearly exactly how everything works.

These technical matters may seem a little difficult and tedious. You may think that you want to simply make movies, not be a camera technician. But your camera is the tool that executes your ideas. If you don't know how to work it properly, you will not be able to get your ideas down on film as easily and exactly as you would like. Therefore, it is definitely worth a little time and practice, and perhaps an experimental roll of film, to become familiar with your camera.

The Tripod

A tripod is simply a three-legged stand to which your camera is attached. The legs will telescope so that when not in use it is easy to carry about. It is a most practical way of holding your camera steady. It is not an essential piece of equipment, but you'll find that any shot made with the camera on a tripod will appear more even and steady when projected than one made with a hand-held camera. You probably won't use it if you are on the move or if you are rushing to catch a passing scene. But

Here is the tripod being used. It is especially handy for very close-up shots.

it is very useful for close-ups and for telephoto shots where any camera movement is greatly magnified. It is essential for animation. You'll also find that people will immediately think you an expert and an old pro once you set up a camera on a tripod. This may be useful if you want to impress your actors or elicit awed or admiring glances from passersby!

Film

In the discussion of cameras we mentioned the different sizes and "packages" that film comes in — on a roll, in a magazine, or in a cartridge. However there are different *kinds* of film.

The most common kind of film used today is color. It is priced just very slightly higher than black-and-white. And color is so widely used you might even have trouble finding a camera store that has black-and-white movie film to sell.

Daylight is bluish in color; artificial light or movie lights have a yellowish cast. Because of this, color film is made in two types — one for use in daylight, one for artificial light. The artificial-light film is called Type A ("A" for artificial). If you

20

have a Super 8 camera you don't have to worry about this distinction. All Super 8 movie film is Type A. These cameras have a filter placed between film and lens which lets you use the Type A film in daylight. When you attach movie lights to the camera, the filter is automatically pushed out of the way. If the lights are not attached directly to the camera, you must use a special little key, which is supplied with the camera, that will push aside the filter.

If you have an 8mm camera you will have to specify when you buy your film whether you want Type A or daylight. If you happened to have Type A film in your camera and decide to shoot in daylight, you can get a filter which will fit over the lens.

There are several other types of special-purpose films, but these are usually available only for Super 8 cameras. One very useful film is high speed and will let you take pictures in very dimly lit situations. You can find out more about these films at any camera store. But for general purposes, a film like Kodachrome II will do fine.

When you buy your film, you can usually buy at the same time what is called a photo-process mailer. This is simply an

A subway station scene like this would appear a dark mass of shadows if shot with conventional movie film. The lighting is very dim—only a few scattered fluorescent lights are in the ceiling. However, fine results can be obtained using one of the newly perfected high-speed films.

envelope. When your film is exposed, put it in this mailer and send it off. This will save you the time and bother of taking the film to a camera store to be developed. It will be returned to you within ten days, on a reel, ready to be projected.

The Projector and Screen

Just as cameras come in a variety of sizes and shapes, with or without many special features, so do projectors. The newer projectors have a self-threading mechanism. This is not an essential feature, but it does save a lot of time and fumbling. With self-threading projectors it is important that the leader film (this is the blank white film at the start of a roll) be properly trimmed, and not bent or twisted. Some projectors have a built-in trimmer which cuts the end of the film into the proper shape for self-threading.

Needless to say, the projector you use must be designed for the film you use. A 16mm projector won't take 8mm film, though there are some projectors that will take both 8mm and Super 8.

Some of the other features that most projectors have are: a variable speed control, a reverse switch, and a "still" control. This will stop the film and show just one frame. The film should never be stopped to show just one frame unless the projector is designed to do this. The intense heat of the projector bulb would burn the film unless a heat-absorbent filter was inserted between bulb and film.

There are also sound projectors. These project sound film, which is a little beyond the scope of the beginning filmmaker. This sort of projector is, as you would expect, a good deal more expensive than the usual silent projector. There are, however, various ways of using sound with your movies, and this is discussed in some detail in chapter 11.

It is possible to project your films on a blank white wall, or even on a white bed sheet. But you will not get as brilliant an image as on a movie screen. The screen is made with a special surface which is designed to get the best possible picture. The most common type of screen has a beaded surface. But there are other types of various designs in a wide range of prices. Most screens are built so that they unroll and then stand upright on a small three-legged base.

At first glance, most projectors look alike. But, like cameras, there are many different features to look for. Some projectors are self-threading, some can show sound film; others have zoom lenses so that the size of the projected picture can vary.

Bauer

Honeywell Elmo

Bell and Howell

Bell and Howell

2. Using the Camera

Like any tool, a camera can be used well or poorly. Different ways of handling the camera and various kinds of shots are discussed in this chapter.

The most important thing about using a camera is to hold it steady. If you jiggle your camera as you are filming, the resulting scene, when projected, will be difficult to watch and very annoying. It is a basic and very important rule that the camera be held as steady as possible.

The camera is usually held as shown in the illustration below. Notice that the hands are close to the body, the legs slightly apart. When there is something to lean against, that will help you keep the camera steady. Sitting down, when possible, also helps. If you put your camera on a tripod you can be sure it will be absolutely steady.

A firm stance and a steady grip are needed to avoid an image that jiggles about on the screen.

How Long to Shoot

The kind of action you are shooting will often determine how long a scene should be. Suppose you were making a film about a football game. If you were shooting a runner with the ball, heading down the field, you would want to keep the scene going for as long as it took him to make a goal or get tackled. In other words, the dramatic action itself would determine the length of the scene. If you were shooting the crowd cheering, you could make this any length you chose.

As with most of the other techniques discussed in this chapter, you should try for variety. Have some scenes very brief, others longer. There is no rule about length of scene. You must try to suit it to the mood and action of what you are filming. Movies have been made using one scene throughout its entire length. Other films have been made using a very quick succession of short scenes, none lasting more than a few seconds. In general, a scene that lasts eight or ten seconds is considered a long scene.

If your camera has a spring motor, rather than an electric motor, you must be sure it is fully wound before shooting any scene. Otherwise, the motor may run down, and what you intended to be a long scene will become a short scene — perhaps with the essential dramatic moment missed. Actually, the length of time a spring motor will run on a winding will determine how long your longest scene can be.

Panning

This means to swing your camera across a scene. Panning is used to follow a subject that is moving across your field of view. It is also used to cover a wide scene that is too broad to be covered in one shot. In this latter case it is very important that the camera be swung *very slowly*. Otherwise the scene is blurred and distorted. Practice panning shots, keeping your feet slightly apart and slowly swinging from the waist. A little practice will enable you to develop a very even, smooth motion.

When you are following a moving object, it is not as vital that the camera motion be perfectly slow and smooth. It isn't that important if the background is blurred, as long as your

The only way to keep the two boys and the dog in view in a scene like this is by panning the camera. Otherwise, the action would have swiftly passed in front of the camera before you could get a good look at it.

subject is clear and sharp. Next time you watch a movie look for panning shots. You will notice that the motion is very slow if the camera is shooting a landscape or panoramic scene. But if the camera is following a horse and rider passing in front of the camera, for example, the camera may pan swiftly, and the background will be blurred, but the horse and rider will remain sharp.

Beginning filmmakers will sometimes direct the camera like a water hose, trying to include everything in front of them. They will point up, down, swing one way, then another, and the resulting projected scene will give everybody a headache. "Motion pictures" means that something is in motion — but not necessarily the camera. Needless to say, the camera often does have to be in motion — as in the case of the passing horse and rider — but unnecessary or erratic motion is to be avoided at all costs.

Near and Far

Most beginning filmmakers don't give much thought to how close or how far away they are from their subject. They will either back away or move in closer until the image in the viewfinder seems about right. The trouble with this method of filming is that you usually don't get much variety. If you make a *conscious* effort to shoot from a variety of distances, your movies will be much more interesting to look at. For the sake of convenience, professional moviemakers refer to three main types of shots. These indicate distance of camera to subject.

THE CLOSE-UP   This kind of shot shows details. It closes in on the essential element in a scene. A close-up of something

This is a close-up with the camera concentrating on one detailed action.

Here we have a medium shot.

This is a long shot. It tells us something about the setting and action. It is an overall view.

27

will not only make it more understandable, it will make it more dramatic. The object you are closing in on is being singled out for your camera's (and the audience's) attention, and this immediately gives it more importance. For example, the camera might close in on a glove that a burglar left behind. The very fact that the camera moves in on this incriminating bit of evidence makes it significant. We know right away that that glove is going to lead to something important in the story.

The camera that has a zoom lens can single out something in a large scene. By slowly and steadily zooming in on one element it can very dramatically point out what you think needs emphasizing.

THE MEDIUM SHOT   In general, when your camera is anywhere between six and twenty feet away from your main subject, you are shooting a medium shot.

THE LONG SHOT   As the name implies, the camera is some distance away from the scene in this kind of a shot. The long shot is often used at the start of a film sequence. It will show the general, overall view. It will often introduce the setting of the action.

The zoom lens is a great aid in getting a variety of shots without dashing back and forth with the camera. With the zoom lens you can shoot a long shot, then adjust your lens, and a moment later be shooting a close-up of the same scene.

Different Angles

This is still another way of getting variety into your films. Any subject can be viewed from many different angles. For example, suppose you wanted to take a sequence of somebody painting a picture. Just one, long, continuous shot, from one point of view, might be interesting for a few seconds, but after a while it would begin to get boring — unless the action itself was so exciting and vivid that the audience would be held spellbound. The rather limited action involved in painting a picture could be made more interesting by using a number of different camera angles and emphasizing different aspects of the action. The illustrations on the opposite page show how this could be done.

28

The Subjective Camera

This rather fancy name refers to a particular style or manner of using the camera. The "subjective camera" means that the camera takes the place of your eye, or your actor's eye. As you walk down the street, for example, the camera might glance about, seeing whatever you would be seeing.

There is a classic use of the "subjective camera" in a film made some years ago. It describes how an injured person is taken out of an ambulance and wheeled down a hospital corridor. The camera is always looking upward, as the patient would be looking. First you see the ceiling of the ambulance. Then there is some jiggling about (the stretcher being removed from the ambulance), then you see the top of a doorway, then the ceiling of the hospital corridor. You see the light fixtures, and at one point a nurse bends over, and her hand reaches down as if to wipe a sweating forehead.

This scene must have been filmed with the camera actually placed on a stretcher and handled just as if it were the patient — with the camera running all the time. You might make an entire movie using this "subjective camera" style, or you might want to use it at only certain times.

The Dolly Shot

This very exotic-sounding shot is useful and great fun to make. The term "dolly" refers to a wagon, or dolly, or any wheeled vehicle which can move the camera in the course of a shot. The illustration below shows the making of a dolly shot. The cameraman is being wheeled along in a shopping cart, keeping pace with the walking actor. In a dolly shot, the camera can stay the same distance from the subject, even as the subject moves. The camera could also be dollied in closer, or away from the subject. This would have the same effect as a zoom shot.

Here is a dolly shot being made. The dolly used here is not a very professional looking piece of equipment, but the scene, when projected on the screen, will have a very professional look indeed. Many film-makers use dolly shots as often as they can. They like to keep their camera moving because they know that it is one way of adding excitement and visual interest to almost any scene.

Hollywood movies often use this kind of shot. Very heavy, rubber-wheeled vehicles carry the camera and cameraman. Often a length of track is laid over uneven ground so that the dolly can roll smoothly.

When you use your camera this way, make sure that your dolly moves along fairly even, smooth ground. A bumpy ride for the cameraman will make a jiggly, hard-to-watch image on the screen.

Another kind of dolly shot can be made from a moving automobile. If you can get someone to drive slowly along as

31

This is the sort of picture you might get, shooting out of the window of a moving car. The constantly changing view would give you a sense of the busy, crowded activity along a city street. This same view would not be nearly as interesting if the camera remained in one place.

you point the camera out the window you will be able to get some extremely interesting shots. Suppose you wanted a scene with some running. You could get something quite dramatic if you were shooting while the car kept pace with the runner. Street scenes, the countryside, and many other views which might not be very interesting if shot from a fixed point of view can become quite effective if shot from a moving vehicle.

Backgrounds

The beginning filmmaker is often so interested in the action in front of his camera that he forgets all about the background. After the film has been processed and returned and projected

A much less cluttered background is obtained by moving the wheelbarrow a few feet to the left. You must always be aware of what is going on behind your subject.

a few times he realizes that there are lots of distracting or ugly goings-on directly behind his subject.

Very often a background can be improved simply by shifting your position a little to change the angle from which you are shooting. If you kneel down and shoot upwards you can get the sky in the background. Or if you get up high and shoot down you can get an area of grass or pavement behind your subject.

Contrast is another thing to think about when it comes to backgrounds. If your subject is in the sun, for example, and the background is in shadow, you will immediately have a dramatic contrast. The same kind of contrast is possible if the background is light and the action in the foreground in shadow. In both cases, the subject is separated from the background, and you get a more effective image.

The contrast between the hot dog stand in the sun and the surrounding, shadowed buildings makes this a dramatic setting.

3. Making a Simple One-Reel Movie

Now that you know something about your camera (Chapter I) and how to use it (Chapter II), you are all set to make a movie. Don't attempt anything complicated or too ambitious for your first effort. Keep your action out-of-doors, so you won't have to worry about odd lighting conditions. Don't assemble a "cast of thousands." They will either get in your way, or someone who thinks he knows it all will proceed to tell you what to do! Something simple, like the afternoon hike described here, is an ideal beginning project. (The next chapter discusses different kinds of films. If you are stuck for an idea, read that chapter now.)

The particular little movie which is illustrated on the following pages is intended to show in an actual situation some of the different ways of using the camera in order to get an interesting variety of scenes. The film was made in a very direct way. There was no cutting, no editing. No zooming, dollying, or special techniques were used. (In chapter 12 there is a description of the making of a longer, more sophisticated film which uses some of the more advanced and experimental skills available to the filmmaker.)

This film, which used just one roll of film, is about a spring afternoon hike through the woods, up a trail to the top of a small mountain.

In a film like this, with a logical sequence of events, there is no need for cutting. The scenes evolve in a natural order. The first scene—getting out of the car—is logically followed by starting up the trail, then eventually reaching the summit, lunch, back down the trail, into the car, and off. This is the order in which these things happened—and if you shoot film along the way, everything will appear in the proper sequence. The only alteration to the final film might be the elimination of poor shots, wrong exposures, etc. If you shot more than one roll, you would have to splice it all together. (Splicing is explained on page 60.)

1. Getting out of the car. A long shot.

2. Starting up the trail. Another long shot.

3. Close-up of trail blaze.

4. Along the trail.

35

5. An extreme close-up.

6. A little variety.

7. The trail gets steeper.

8. A pause to rest. Close-up.

9. A dramatic spot.

10. Close-up.

11. Nearing the top. A different angle.

12. A pan shot with figures in foreground.

13. Eating.

14. . . . and drinking. A close-up.

15. Then starting back down.

16. Coming down. A different angle.

17. The end of the trail.

18. Tired hikers.

4. "What Kind of Movie Can I Make?"

This chapter discusses the different approaches to filmmaking. There are a great many different kinds of movies to be made. In fact, there are as many ideas about moviemaking as there are moviemakers. In general, amateur films are much more varied and offbeat than films made by commercial companies. Hollywood worries about satisfying an audience of millions. Television films worry about keeping their ratings up so that sponsors can sell their wares.

The amateur filmmaker has only himself to satisfy. He is selling nothing; his audience is himself, his friends and relatives. He can do absolutely anything he feels like doing.

The basic types of films are described here. But in actual practice you'll find that a film will often fit into two or more categories.

The Travelogue

This sort of movie is a record of places visited. Most movies made on vacation trips are travelogues. They are probably the most frequently made movies. They will show where you've been, what you did there, what happened en route. When a travelogue is made with thought and care it can be great fun.

Below and on the next page are a few scenes that might be included in a movie about a visit to the Statue of Liberty. The statue is a handsome object—large, colorful, historically important. But you wouldn't get a very interesting movie by merely taking a series of shots of the statue itself. To make an entertaining film you need shots of the boat trip to the statue, what you and your friends did, the crowds of people, the souvenirs, the New York City skyline, as well as views of the statue. The particular sequence of shots reproduced here concentrates more on the trip than on the statue itself.

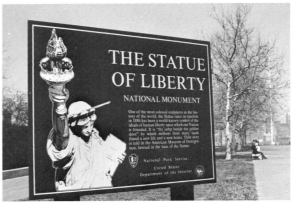

When it is only a jumble of panoramic views of landscapes and monuments with someone standing stiffly in the foreground, it will be a great yawn-producer.

If you can think of this type of movie as a story, as well as a travelogue, you will be off to a good start. Shoot a few scenes of the preparations for the trip—more packing, looking at maps, getting in the car or plane, or whatever the means of transportation is. Then devote some footage to each of the activities you want to record. If you spend an afternoon fishing, make a little subplot of that—getting in the boat, baiting the hook, casting, a catch, removing the hook, returning, cooking the fish, etc. Then shift to another activity, handling that in some detail, and so on, ending with your return home.

On any vacation trip there are bound to be some scenes you will want to record—the Statue of Liberty, Yosemite Falls, an Indian snake dance, etc.—which you can't very well make a personal story of. In these cases, you must use your artistic judgment and imagination to get the most interesting and attractive shots. Use varied angles, close-ups, telephoto shots. Keep shifting your position so you can get different views. If possible, have your friends or family walking or climbing through the scene. Have them reacting or participating in some way. If you have a view too large to include in a simple, straight shot, pan the camera, remembering to swing it very, very slowly.

The Special Event Film

This is another very common type of movie. It serves to record some special occasion—dressing the Christmas tree, Graduation Day, Aunt Harriet from South America comes for a visit, someone builds an eight-foot snowman, a wedding, etc. It is great fun to look at this sort of film years later and recall good times and happy memories. However, it is sometimes a bit of a challenge to make this kind of thing interesting to people other than the participants.

Here again it is best to avoid having people standing and posing. Have them doing something. Give some thought beforehand to what is going to be happening so that you will be ready to shoot the most important action. Try to get a sequence of scenes that will have some continuity as well as dramatic interest. Have a beginning and an end. Use a variety of shots.

Suppose you wanted to make a record of the eight-foot snowman—how could you make anything interesting out of that? The trick would be to get a sequence of scenes showing the actual construction of the snowman, rather than just a quick snapshot of the finished product. You might start with a shot of someone looking out the window and seeing snow. Then, putting on boots, making a snowball, a close-up of snowball, rolling a bigger snowball, perhaps slipping and falling, piling one snowball on another, filling gaps, other people helping, maybe a neighbor's dog will come to investigate, setting up a stepladder, etc. What you would be doing, in effect, is making a little story or drama out of a simple episode.

The Story

Any series of events which fit together can make a story. The story doesn't necessarily have to have a plot with a trick ending. It doesn't have to be the sort of story where boy meets girl, or map is found in attic—treasure-pirates-escape, etc. That sort of thing is certainly a story and perfectly fine. But it can be much simpler.

As long as there is a sequence of events—one logically developing out of the other—and leading up to some kind of climax, you have the basic structure of a story.

Let's take an example of a not very extraordinary event and see how it could be made into a movie story. Suppose you had a friend who was going to buy a new bike. The outline below shows one way of handling this simple activity so that it could be made into a story with a beginning, a middle, and a climax.
1. You might start with a shot of the old bike in some kind of trouble—breaking down, brakes failing, parts falling off, or something of the sort.
2. Your friend looking angry or annoyed.
3. Looking at a bicycle catalogue.
4. Getting the money for a new bike somehow—maybe doing odd jobs, babysitting, etc.
5. Shopping for the new bike—visiting different stores, examining different bikes.

6. Buying the bike.

7. Taking it out of the store and riding happily off.

This outline could be the basis for a short or fairly lengthy movie. Number four could be a whole subplot with all sorts of adventures and misadventures involved in earning the needed money. But, whatever way it is handled, it is a *story* because all the individual scenes would be building up toward the climax when the bike is purchased and pedaled off.

If you feel that you'd like to make a movie with a story but—even after a lot of head-scratching—you can't find any suitable ideas, think of some of the more interesting things that have

Many amateur filmmakers start out with one or two characters, making up the story as they go along. This will sometimes result in a confusing plot, but if there are interesting settings, lots of vigorous action, and the actors use a little imagination and humor, the results can be great fun.

happened to you or your friends. Or think of some of the novels or short stories you've read, or movies or TV shows you've seen. This should produce some ideas. Don't hesitate to change, switch around, or completely re-do any of the ideas you find this way. In fact, you will probably have to, whether you want to or not.

Make changes to simplify your shooting. Don't be concerned that the original story was set along the banks of the upper Amazon, or in the fifteenth century. Cut out what you don't want or can't handle. Change settings to suit your own ideas, add or remove characters as you wish. Perhaps your *Romeo and Juliet* will end up as a story of two puppies lost in a big city—no matter, if it is a story that you've enjoyed making and that has turned out well.

There is one thing you must bear in mind when you are planning a movie with a story; your actors will not be heard talking. Although you can add sound with a phonograph or a tape recorder (see chapter 11), you will not be able to synchronize voice with lip movement unless you are lucky enough to have the use of some very fancy, expensive, sound-film equipment. In other words, remember that you are making "silents," not "talkies." Therefore your story cannot depend on dialogue. The visual action itself will have to explain what is going on.

For example, let's suppose a character is sitting on a bench waiting for a bus which has been delayed. If you had Hollywood sound equipment, you could have your actor say, "I reckon that dang ol' bus is late!" But shooting a silent film, you would probably have your actor look at his watch, glance up the road, and then maybe spit out a wad of tobacco juice in disgust. In both cases the meaning would be perfectly clear.

With a little thought you'll find that you can convey most meanings by purely visual means. Getting your ideas across this way is often a great challenge—and very satisfying when you get it to work well.

Horror Movies

Many people have an enormous amount of fun with this kind of movie. These movies are modeled on ideas like *Dracula, Frankenstein, Vampire Bat Meets the Zombies, King Kong in the Swimming Pool, The Monster From the Deep*

Freeze, etc. The cornier and more outrageous the better, and they turn out to be fine comedies.

It will be helpful if you can get some of the dreadful-looking, rubber Halloween-type masks that some novelty stores sell. Or you can simply run wild with makeup: scars, black shadows around the eyes, false noses, odd twisting limps, and so on. Maybe you can borrow an old wig from somebody. And don't neglect to assemble as peculiar a collection of clothing as possible.

The plots of this kind of movie don't have to be very subtle—or even very clear! Chases, mysterious devices, spying, hidden treasures, and the like are possibilities. You can greatly improve your movie with good settings. Decaying houses, dark and sinister woods, strange rocky cliffs, etc. would be much more suitable than your back yard.

Thematic Movies

This kind of movie takes a simple, basic idea or theme and explores it. For example, you could put together a film of almost any length on themes like: heat, loneliness, traffic, eating, the color yellow, leisure, snow time, being tired, reflections on the water, football, and so on.

Suppose you choose a theme—speed. How would you build a film around this idea? You might start out with something moving slowly, like leaves in the wind, then perhaps surf crashing on a beach, the whirling gears of an engine of some kind, trains, a skier rushing downhill, a stopwatch—maybe a sudden contrast of somebody sprawled out sleeping—then feet running, a bicycle coasting downhill with the camera pointing at the ground as it flashes by, etc. Once you choose a theme and start thinking about it, all kinds of ideas will come to you until you find you have all the material you could possibly use.

The theme in a thematic movie doesn't have to be unusual or extraordinary. Shots like those shown here could be used in a film about the city. You could concentrate on just one aspect of city life—the people, or their activities, their businesses, their clothing. Or, you might want to make a film that shows textures, details, odd angles, or scenes of the city's architecture. How about a film about animals in the city, or city travel, or different neighborhoods?

The Portrait

A movie that is concerned with one person is a portrait film; you might prefer to call it a biography. This kind of movie can tell you a good deal about a person—what he does, how he spends his time, where he goes, what he eats, what his room is like. You can go into as much or as little detail as you like. It can be a biography of anyone—a grandparent, friend, brother, or even yourself.

How about doing a portrait of a pet? You could use a title like, "A Day in the Life of Bozo."

The Science Essay

This kind of movie is often useful in connection with some sort of research project. If you are interested in forestry, geology, ecology, botany, etc., you can use the camera to record much useful information. You might be able to show how a footbridge is built, where a certain kind of bird builds its nest, how a beach erodes, what kinds of trees grow in what environments, how a house is built, etc. On the next page are scenes you might find in a film explaining the construction of a model boat.

You may be able to record certain types of laboratory experiments. Slow-motion photography will show clearly how a rocket blasts off, how a horse runs, how a high jumper lands. Time-lapse photography (see page 84.) will show how a fern opens, how frost forms on a window pane, how a skyscraper grows . . .

The many different steps in the building of a steam-powered model tugboat such as the one shown here would provide the material for a very interesting science essay. Most movies that show the growth, development, and completion of some kind of construction project are informative as well as entertaining, though a film of this sort usually requires a spoken commentary to explain what is going on. This particular model was built in a shop that had a large skylight, providing a strong but diffused light that is excellent for all kinds of picture taking. Notice how an effort was made to eliminate clutter and confusion from the background. The final scene shows the finished model in operation.

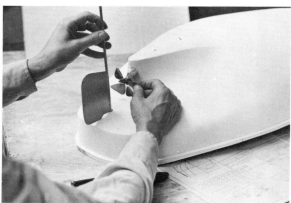

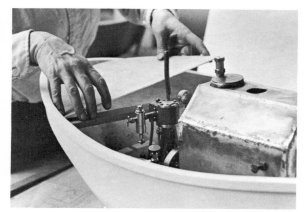

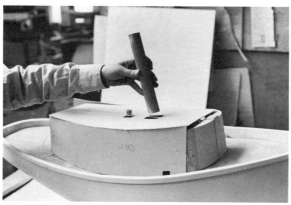 

The Impressionist Movie

This is a loose category similar to that of thematic films. It includes the filming of unplanned scenes which for one reason or another appeal to the filmmaker. He hopes that he can fit them all together to make an interesting sequence of visual images. It is an intuitive, poetic way of working. Sometimes the results are jumpy and disconnected, sometimes smoothly related because of color, motion, shapes, and moods.

Social Comment

Movies are often made for the purpose of expressing an opinion about something. When a film is made to show and describe a condition which is dangerous, or ugly, or unfair, the simple act of showing these conditions to an audience has the implicit question, "Don't you think this is a poor state of affairs? And don't you think something can be done about it?"

If everybody thinks your town is perfect, with no slums, and you make a film showing poor families living in shacks on the edge of town, you are making a strong statement suggesting that there is a need for low-income housing.

There are certainly many things in our society which could stand improvement, and you, as a filmmaker, can make your ideas known to anybody who sees the films you make.

Here are some scenes that would fit well in films about pollution and overpopulation.

Animation

This is a completely different kind of filmmaking. It incorporates a good many of the ideas and possibilities mentioned here, but the technique is so different that a separate chapter is devoted to it.

5. Planning Your Movie

The Need for Planning

There should always be some kind of planning before you start out to make a movie. One reason is economic. Film and processing are not inexpensive, and there is less chance of wasted scenes and useless footage if you have a plan.

Another reason is that you may suddenly remember—when it is too late—that you neglected to shoot some important part of your film. This can easily happen if you don't have some kind of plan to go by.

Another reason—and a very important one—is that most movies should have a sense of continuity. They should progress from one scene to the next in a logical way.

There are different kinds of "relatedness," or continuity. For example in the shooting list on page 53, scene 2 is related to scene 3. In scene 17 our actress gets out of the bus. In scene 3 she looks about. One action follows logically and dramatically after the other. There is continuity.

In another example you might show surf breaking on a beach, followed by a shot of a seagull flying overhead. Both scenes are about the seashore and so fit together.

Another example might be a shot of a red, flashing light on a fire engine, and then a scene of a red sunset. The two kinds of red light would provide a relationship.

A *contrast* is another kind of relatedness. Suppose you had a shot of some racing speedboats, and then a scene of a man lying in bed, fast asleep. There would be a certain logical continuity because of the violent contrasts of these two actions.

Different kinds of movies require different kinds of planning. If you are making an impressionist movie—one that is concerned with mood and shapes and colors, you can set out with only the faintest idea of what you are going to shoot. You may have a theme—loneliness, the city, rushing, shopping, wintertime, or whatever—but you don't know until you begin to explore just which scene will convey your thought and and feelings. You may simply wander about shooting whatever catches your fancy and seems to fit in with your theme. When you have shot a few rolls like this you will probably have to do a great deal of editing. You will probably want to switch scenes about, cutting and fitting to make a coherent movie where the scenes relate well to one another.

Many very effective movies have been made this way which capture vivid, poetic, and often very beautiful moods and feelings. The trouble is that often much of the film that you've shot doesn't logically fit and has to be discarded (. . . or put aside to be used elsewhere).

If your movie idea is based upon a story, you have to plan a little more carefully. You should make a list of some kind— a reminder list or "shooting list"—to make sure you don't forget anything important. This kind of list can also simplify your shooting.

Suppose someone in your story walks through a certain door in a city. Then, after many other scenes elsewhere, the same person is supposed to go back in that door. It would simplify things enormously if you shot the two scenes, one after the other, at the same time. Then you wouldn't have to return to that location later. The second scene could be cut out of the processed film when you did your editing and spliced in where it belonged.

If you had a shooting list you could tell at a glance that these two scenes could be shot at the same time. Without a list you might—or might not—realize that this could be done. When you have a shooting list you can shoot the scenes you want for your film in any sequence, at any time . . . and then put it all in the proper sequence when you do your editing.

The shooting list opposite is an example of one you might prepare before starting to make a film. It serves not only as a shooting guide, but as a sort of story outline.

STRANGER IN TOWN

Scene 1. Bus pulling into terminal.

Scene 2. Elizabeth gets off, carrying guitar.

Scene 3. Close-up of Elizabeth. She looks around.

Scene 4. Shot of buildings.

Scene 5. Several shots of very busy traffic—cabs, buses, trucks. (Use telephoto lens.)

Scene 6. Elizabeth walks away, merging into crowd on sidewalk.

Scene 7. Waiting on corner for light to change, then crossing. (Telephoto.)

Scene 8. Close-up of wheels of traffic, or hurrying feet. (Several very brief shots.)

Scene 9. Elizabeth stands on corner, looking puzzled. (Use telephoto and shoot from a distance.)

Scene 10. She asks passerby for directions.

Scene 11. She stops at street vendor and buys hot dog.

Scene 12. Eating hot dog. (Close-up.)

Scene 13. Strolling along, eating hot dog. (Long shot.)

Scene 14. She stops to look into store window. (Shoot from inside store.)

Scene 15. Walking along the street. (Several shots of this from different angles and distances.)

Scene 16. She crosses another street and sits down on a bench in the park. There is another girl on bench. (Long shot.)

Scene 17. Elizabeth looking at other girl. (Medium shot.)

Scene 18. Other girl reaches behind bench and picks up guitar.

Scene 19. Elizabeth grins. (Close-up.)

Scene 20. They both start to play guitars. (Medium shot.)

Scene 21. Same scene from farther away.
Scene 22. Same scene from still farther away.
(Or zoom away.)
Scene 23. Same scene. (Slowly pan camera away from bench to get close-up of hurrying feet or heavy traffic moving by in a rush.)

With a list like this, you are ready to go out and start filming. The list represents your general plan of action, and as you shoot each scene, check it off. Most of the scenes listed here are fairly general, and there is no reason in the world you have to shoot each one. You may change your mind and completely change the story as you go along. As you are filming this story you might run into all kinds of unexpected backgrounds or events that might help the story. Perhaps there will be a traffic accident, or a sudden rainstorm, or a parade. Some of the action listed is unpredictable. You can't be sure of the kinds of street crowds you will encounter. Maybe there won't be a hot-dog vendor. Perhaps the street traffic will be light. But with your list in hand you have at least some idea of what you want to achieve, and you can make substitutions as needed.

A method that many serious filmmakers use is to describe each scene beforehand on a separate 3- by 5-inch file card. The card might look something like this:

Scene 7: Elizabeth is waiting on corner, ready to cross the street. She is looking around, uncertain. Shoot from far side of street, starting about three or four seconds before light changes and she proceeds to cross. Stay behind car or lamp post so camera won't be seen by the people approaching. Use telephoto. (About 10-15 seconds.)

This is a very elaborate kind of notation and you must visualize the movie ahead of time in rather complete detail. The cards will also be helpful after the film is shot when you do the editing. You can jot down on each card any changes you want to make.

Working With Others

One person, working by himself, can make almost any kind of film. But it is nice to work with someone else on a movie. When two or more people sit down together and begin talking about film ideas, it is only a question of minutes before all kinds of suggestions, stories, plans, and projects are considered. The give-and-take of conversation with several people will spark many ideas.

Companions in filmmaking are useful in many practical ways. There will be instances where you and your friends will take turns acting and working the camera. When lights have to be held or the camera dollied, an additional hand is very welcome.

However, there is also the danger of too many bosses. When there are several people involved in making a movie, there will certainly be several points of view. This is fine if there is discussion and everybody agrees on what has to be done. But if there are continuous arguments and a conflict of ideas, you will have to figure out a way of working together. The simplest solution is to take turns being the director. Each person would have a chance to be the director for one reel or one scene.

6. Editing

Editing is the process of cutting a roll of film apart to eliminate what you don't want, or to change the order of what you want to keep. The actual cutting with scissors and then rejoining of the film is called "splicing." It is not difficult and is explained at the end of the chapter.

The simplest kind of editing is to splice two or more rolls of film into one long roll which can be shown without interruption. When you have an audience, it is best to avoid showing many short, 50-foot reels. You'll be rethreading film and rewinding half the time, and your audience will get restless. Try to have your films on a 400-foot reel—even if there are several different, unrelated movies spliced together.

Another kind of editing is to remove mistakes. When your film is returned from the processor it is exactly the way it was taken. It is on a reel ready to be projected. If there were no errors of exposure, if the camera was always properly focused, if the camera never jiggled, or if the action never moved out of the frame—if everything was exactly right—you can just pop the film into the projector whenever you want to show it, and that is the end of the entire filmmaking process.

But very few rolls of film are perfect. There is usually something that can be eliminated. This kind of editing is simple, with few decisions to worry over. You simply snip out what you want to get rid off, then splice the remaining ends together.

But there is another kind of editing which is not done to remove errors, but rather to alter the length of scenes, and to alter their sequence. It is used to build a rhythm and pattern that can vastly increase the dramatic interest of a movie. Let's take an example and see how editing can create an exciting situation.

Suppose you are making a movie in which a thief, fleeing someone, runs across some railroad tracks. You could take several shots of your actor running—long shots, close-ups, from different angles. Then you could take a variety of other shots, an approaching locomotive, freight cars, lights reflecting on steel tracks, overhead power lines, semaphores, close-ups of train wheels. (See next two pages.)

In order to build up tension and excitement you must have these various shots in a sequence that will produce this feeling. The obvious thing would be to jump quickly from one shot to another, and to have them get shorter and shorter as the action progressed. Finally there would be a climax, and the thief would either escape or get captured.

By cutting and splicing your film you can get the sequence and tempo you want. This is the most creative kind of editing and can have a great deal to do with whether a film is boring or exciting. The editors who work on professional films are considered among the most important people in the industry—almost on a par with the director in some instances.

The illustrations on page 59 show one possible sequence of shots from our "thief-crossing-the-tracks" epic. Unfortunately, there is no way of showing in a book the different lengths of the scenes. So you will have to try and visualize the tempo gradually increasing as the action comes to a climax and then changes into the next scene. When a complicated scene like this is edited you have a lot of cutting and splicing to do.

Look at your film many times. Make notes about the changes you want to make. Then cut the film apart and tape or pin it up on a wall, or place it in small containers. Make a brief note on a scrap of paper to identify each piece of film. Without these little labels you'll get hopelessly confused. Then place all the pieces of film in the order in which they are to go. Now

On this page we have on the left the thief running down the tracks, then a series of shots of trains and various sights along the way.

With careful editing, the railroad scenes can be interspersed with the running figure to build up a feeling of excitement and danger.

you are ready to start splicing. (Don't try to do too much editing at one time. An hour or two-hour session of editing is plenty. More than that and it will stop being fun and you'll begin to lose your patience.)

There are some scenes and some kinds of action where you can do the editing in the camera. This means that you shoot in the proper sequence and for the proper length of time for each bit of action. You might take a quick shot of the thief, then one of the tracks, then another of the thief, another of the tracks, the approaching locomotive, and so on. If you can get what you want this way it is fine and will save you a good deal of cutting and splicing.

However, there can be problems. Suppose, for example, there is only one train a day that passes over these tracks. You will have only one chance to photograph that train. If you frantically jump back and forth between thief, semaphore, tracks, train, etc., you probably won't get the kind of shots you want of *any* of these things. You will be rushing too fast to be able to work carefully.

After you've been making movies for some time, you'll find you have a good deal of leftover or discarded film. It could be entire rolls you don't like, or scraps and snippets left over from your editing. See if you can assemble this miscellaneous material into some kind of sequence. You may end up with something thoroughly disconnected, or you may be able to make some kind of logical combinations. Sometimes the odd relationships can be very funny.

Splicing

You must have a splicer and splicing tape in order to splice film. The splicer is a very simple and inexpensive little gadget, and the tape is like transparent Scotch tape with little holes which line up with the sprocket holes on the film. The first few times you splice you may find it a little awkward. But once you have the hang of it, it is simple and speedy.

There is another way to splice. It is called a wet splice. This involves a different kind of splicer and uses a fast-drying cement. If you happen to have a splicer of this kind you'll have to study it carefully to figure out how it works. Basically, the operation consists of cutting the two edges of the film to be

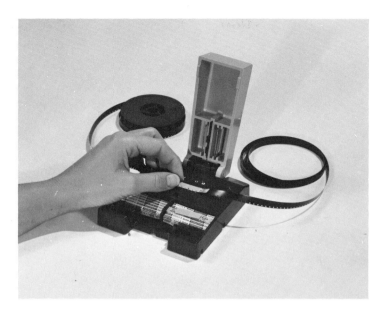

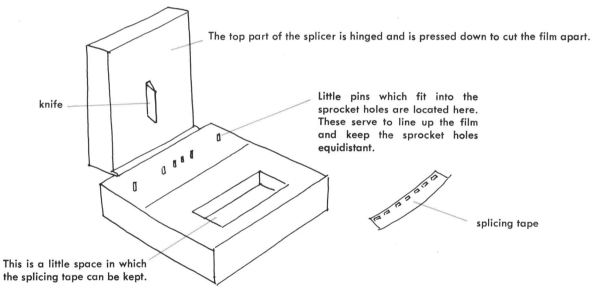

The top part of the splicer is hinged and is pressed down to cut the film apart.

knife

Little pins which fit into the sprocket holes are located here. These serve to line up the film and keep the sprocket holes equidistant.

splicing tape

This is a little space in which the splicing tape can be kept.

joined, scraping the edges clean, painting on a dab of cement, then holding the edges tightly together for fifteen or twenty seconds while the cement is drying. For the beginner, the tape splice is easiest, and quite foolproof.

The tape splice is better for another reason. If you have made a splice and then change your mind and want to un-splice it, all you have to do is carefully peel away the tape.

The Editor

The editing process is faster and easier if you have the use of an editor. This is a little machine that is like a small-scale projector. There is a bulb and a small screen on which the film is viewed. The film is moved by a hand crank. This means that you can slowly go back and forth over a roll of film, examining it as carefully as you want, stopping when you want. Needless to say, before you start cutting film apart, you should be completely familiar with what you have and be clear in your mind about what you intend to do.

If you don't have the use of an editor you will have to use your projector. It is a little troublesome taking the film out, cutting it, then rethreading and continuing on. The only other possibility is to try and hold the film up to the light to see what's going on and where to cut. Since 8mm film is not large, you would have to look carefully.

An editor like this will be a great help when you are editing your films.

7. Light, Location, Color

The image your camera records is determined by the kind of light you have to work with. A bright, sunny day with sharp shadows and strong color has one sort of look and feeling. A day that is overcast, with soft, subdued colors and shadows that are diffused, will be quite different. When you are getting ready to film something, think for a moment about the kind of light that is illuminating your scene. Would you be better off moving from bright sun to a shaded area? Would you gain anything by shifting your position so that the light is coming from

The quality of light on your subject will make an enormous difference in the way it looks. The figure on the left is in direct, glaring sunlight. There are deep, black shadows and strong contrasts. In the other photograph the figure has moved into the shade of the willow tree. Here the light is diffused and softened by the leaves. You can see the face more clearly. Each kind of lighting has its own uses. If, for example, this figure was supposed to be a cruel pirate captain planning something unpleasant, the stark, contrasty lighting might be more appropriate than the softer, more gentle lighting.

63

in front, behind, from the side? Is it better to have a figure in shadow, in glaring light, in a hazy light, lighted from below?

Often you will be concerned with matters more important than light. You will probably be thinking about the action or the position of your camera, or the size and location of your subject. But lighting contributes to the effectiveness of a movie, and on occasion it can be extremely important. It is worth giving some thought.

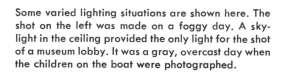

Some varied lighting situations are shown here. The shot on the left was made on a foggy day. A skylight in the ceiling provided the only light for the shot of a museum lobby. It was a gray, overcast day when the children on the boat were photographed.

Don't be afraid to try and capture unusual lighting situations if they appeal to you. In this scene the camera was pointed almost directly into the sun in order to get the glaring reflections on the water.

64

This scene is lit mainly by light coming from the window at which the camera is pointed. There is a very nice quality of light, but it is tricky to get the proper exposure.

Artificial Light

It is not always possible to film out-of-doors where there is plenty of light. (Occasionally you may be able to shoot indoors, near windows, where there is enough natural light.) But sooner or later, you will find you need more light than is available if you are going to be able to shoot what you want. When this happens you need artificial light.

One popular kind of artificial light is a spotlight that attaches directly to the camera. This works well with the newer types of Super 8 cameras, and if you follow the directions that come with the light you should get adequate results. Lights of this sort have a little projection which fits into a slot in the top of the camera. The projection pushes aside the filter which is normally in position between lens and film. With this filter out of the way, the camera can operate in artificial light with no color distortion.

Remember that there is one kind of film for use in daylight, another for artificial light. Super 8 cameras use only artificial-light film, but have a filter that is normally in position. Thus the camera is normally set for daylight use. If you use artificial lights which are *not* attached to the camera, you have to push the filter out of the way by means of a "key." This key comes with the camera.

Two floodlights are being used here to provide the lighting for a close-up shot of someone playing a trumpet. These floodlights, which have built-in reflectors, are attached to light stands and are pointed at the ceiling. The light bounces off the ceiling, spreading about, providing an excellent, soft, overall kind of illumination. A large piece of cardboard has been placed behind the trumpet player so that there will be a plain white background. Notice that the camera is placed on a tripod.

The kind of light which attaches to the camera will provide all the light you need for most situations. But it is a rather unattractive kind of lighting. It is likely to be glaring and rather harsh. A better way to get enough light for indoor shooting is to use one or two photoflood bulbs. These are large, high-wattage bulbs which produce a lot of light. They only last for about six hours, so they shouldn't be left burning needlessly. One very effective way to use these lights is to point them upward toward the ceiling—if it is a white ceiling. This will diffuse the light so that the entire area where you are shooting will have a soft, even light.

If you have a newer camera with an automatic exposure device, the lens opening will be set automatically. You are sure of the proper exposure. If there isn't enough light for proper exposure there will be some kind of warning signal to tell you that more light is needed.

If you have an older camera or a simple one with no automatic exposure-setting mechanism, you will need an exposure meter. This is a gadget that shows how much light there is and tells you what the lens setting should be. The information slip that comes with the film will also tell you proper settings for different artificial light sources.

Here are a few things to remember when you are using artificial light:

Be sure to use artificial-light film. If you happen to have only daylight-type film, you must use the kind of filter that will permit the proper color balance.

If you have a camera without an automatic exposure control, be very cautious about your exposure settings. It is very difficult to make a good guess about the strength of artificial light. An exposure meter is a big help.

If you are taking pictures in a room that is well lit by fluorescent light and you are not using floods or spots, it is possible to use your camera set for daylight exposure. Fluorescent lights usually have a color that is similar to daylight.

When you are using floods or spots be sure that the action you are shooting doesn't move away into some unlit area. You will end up with underexposed scenes.

Watch for glare. Don't let your lights reflect off mirrors or polished surfaces into the lens of your camera.

There have recently been developed some very high-speed color films which greatly simplify shooting under poor light conditions. With these films it is often possible to shoot in quite dimly lit areas with no special lights. The camera store salesman where you buy your film will be able to tell you more about these special films, and whether they can be used in the kind of camera you have. (Try to buy your film in a camera store rather than a drugstore or candy store. Then you'll be able to ask questions or ask for advice and get a knowledgeable reply.)

Sometimes the artificial light is already all set up and arranged for you, as in this shot made in a museum gallery.

Location

In professional filmmaking parlance, being "on location" means being out of the studio—or at some place where the setting is interesting or appropriate. The amateur filmmaker doesn't have any studio, so the question of shooting in the studio or on location never arises, and in some kinds of films the entire question of location doesn't even occur. If you were filming a hiking trip, or a ball game, or comings and goings at an airport, for example, then the location or setting is what your film is all about. All you would do is choose camera angles, actions, sequences, details, and so on.

But very often you do have a choice of location. And what you choose is important and has a lot to do with the interest and excitement of a scene. Let's take an example. Suppose you wanted a close-up of one of your actors, looking frightened. If you were shooting in an open, sunny field, the results would be quite different from shooting in a narrow, dark alley with only a thin beam of light shining down on the actor's face. Even though this was a close-up with the frame filled mostly by the face, there would be enough light or darkness, color and general mood to carry over into the final image and to make a considerable difference.

To take another example, suppose you are making a film where two people accidently meet. Wouldn't it be much more interesting to have your actors meet on a busy street corner, in a train station, on a hilltop, a bridge—rather than in your backyard, or on your front stoop?

It is worth making an effort to find a location that is dramatic, or particularly interesting in some way.

Sometimes a location might be so interesting in itself that you can make an entire movie about it. For example, you might be able to make a movie about what happens on one street corner, or in a school yard, at a gas station, at a farmer's market, in and around a big shade tree, and so on.

Color

Practically all film used today is color film. So color, too, is something to consider. There is no correct or proper way to use it. But if you are aware of color, you'll find that there are

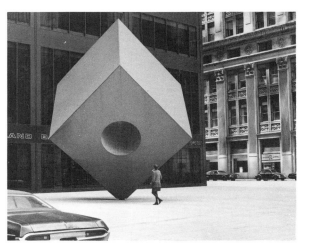

Here are some locations or settings that might add interest to many different kinds of movies. The deserted street might be an appropriate setting for a scene in a spy film. The secret agent might come around a corner, approach the camera, look furtively about, then go off to the right, followed a moment later by the CIA agent who is trailing him on his bike. The barn might be a useful setting in a cowboy and Indian movie. The other locations have an out-of-the-ordinary quality that could provide good settings for a variety of purposes.

It is likely you will see settings and locations that are worth shooting simply because of their interest and beauty, even if they are not suitable as settings for some particular story or project you have in mind. You might decide to make a movie featuring the countryside or landscapes you find most interesting. For example, you could do a film on the Maine coast, or the High Sierras, or U.S. Route 1, and so on. Because movies like this don't usually have too much in the the way of human activity to provide a personal interest you must use your imagination to get varied angles, close-ups, camera motion, etc. in order to avoid a still picture, snap-shot look. A carefully chosen musical background is also very useful.

many changes and choices that you can make. You can choose your backgrounds. You may be able to say something about the clothes your actors are wearing. You may look for subjects which have some particular interest because of color.

There is one movie I've seen that was based solely on the idea of color. The entire film consisted of a great variety of objects, things, scenes that had one color in common—orange. You might see what kind of film you could make using this idea. How about a pink film? A yellow film?

Sometimes your choice of colors can determine the mood of a scene. Suppose you wanted to show the confusion of big-city traffic. A series of brief shots of a yellow cab, a green car, a red stop sign, a bright blue truck, etc. would give the nervous, jumpy, erratic feeling you wanted.

Or suppose you were shooting a scene where the deranged monster paused to catch his breath in front of a wall. That wall might be a plain brown brick wall. But wouldn't it be much more effective if that wall were covered with bright, many-colored, peeling posters (maybe one advertising *Frankenstein Returns*), or perhaps painted a sinister purple or gaudy green? These colors would set a mood and help build suspense.

8. How to Make Titles

Even the shortest movie will be improved if it starts with a title. A title gives a movie a sense of importance and a sense of structure. A well-made title will give your film a professional look.

Titles can be simple or quite elaborate. The simplest kind of title is a shot of some kind of ready-made sign. For example, if you were making a movie about Forty-second Street, what could be more effective than a close-up shot of the street sign itself?

This title has been formed with pine cones. They have been placed so that the shadows along the edges of the cones make the letters more legible.

Transfer letters were pressed onto a piece of white cardboard to spell out this title. Here it is placed amidst a clump of flowers.

You can also make very effective titles by writing with chalk on a wall, scratching the title in the sand, spelling it out with pebbles, stamping it out in the snow, and so on.

More elaborate titles can be made by lettering on a large sheet of white paper or white cardboard. If you don't trust your own lettering, or want to be very neat, it is possible to buy sheets of transfer letters which can be rubbed onto your paper. Most well-stocked art stores will have these.

Another possibility is to use a felt-tip pen to letter your title on a sheet of glass. Then you can hold the glass in front of the camera while the camera is pointed at a suitable background scene. Focus the camera on the lettering—then, after a few seconds, while the camera is still running, shift the focus to

Because the letters are on glass it is possible to have any background you want. This kind of title can be very effective when there is action taking place behind the glass.

the background. You'll probably need someone to help you with this—one person to hold the glass while you hold the camera and adjust the focus. You might also experiment with zooming in on your title if your camera has this kind of lens.

If your film is fairly elaborate, or uses actors, you may want to follow the title shot with a list of your cast. And you will probably want to finish up your production with "The End." (The word "title" applies to more than the name of a film. It also applies to any written material added to a film. For example, foreign movies sometimes have "sub-titles" when the voices aren't dubbed into English. This means that the dialogue appears in English at the bottom of the screen.)

Film titles can be a great deal of fun to make and they can get quite dramatic. In fact, there was one amateur film that consisted of title and nothing else! It was called *Portrait of the Artist as a Young Man,* after the title of a novel by James Joyce. The entire film consisted of the letters of the title appearing one after the other in very imaginative ways. The film started with a boy in a bathing suit walking toward the camera. The camera swung around as he passed, and you then could see the letter *P* painted on his back. This was immediately followed by another scene where somebody scratched the letter *O* on a fogged-up window. The *R* was chalked on a sidewalk, and so on all through the title.

You've probably noticed that many professional films today start with some action, and then, after a brief time, the titles and credits appear. Or the credits are at the very end. You might consider doing this.

This title was lettered on a sheet of white paper, using a brush and black ink.

Many different kinds of props can also be put to good use for titles. Here are a few possibilities: A box is opened and someone slowly pulls out a long strip of paper on which the title is lettered. An object is turned around or turned over, and on the other side you see the title. A line moves along a map (using animation) and arrives where your film has been made, and then the title is spelled out, letter by letter, on the map. One of your actors reaches into his pocket and pulls out a piece of paper, unfolds it, and there is the title. There are an infinite number of ways to make titles with imagination and humor.

The films you make will in most cases be silent. So you might occasionally want to introduce some written comment or explanation. If two objects meet forcibly, a title like the one shown above might be appropriate.

Or something might happen that needs explaining. This would be another reason to use a title. For example; "Ten years later . . ." or "Meanwhile, back at the ranch . . ." or "But Herman didn't know the diamond was glass . . ."

9. Animation

When the term "animation" is used, most people think of cartoons. But cartoons are only one type of animation. There are many other kinds, and most don't require any tricky or specialized equipment or any special talent in art.

The cartoon uses a series of drawings. Each drawing is changed very slightly from the previous one. One frame of film is exposed for each drawing.

When a series of images like these are flashed on the screen one at a time, the eye blends the slight changes together and there is the illusion of a figure walking. In actual practice, it would require something like fifteen or twenty drawings to show the figure taking one step. This is a very slow and tedious way to make an animated film. It also requires specialized tracing equipment to ensure that each drawing is properly positioned in relation to the drawings preceding and following it.

Animated films can be made with other kinds of drawings. You can cut out shapes and move them slightly after each frame of film is exposed, as shown below. You could also make cutout, puppet-type figures or animals with the limbs joined by brass spreader pins.

If your figure is made up of several movable pieces, you don't have to make a separate drawing for each little movement. In this case you only have to slightly shift the elements after each exposure. The horse shown here is composed of ten pieces of stiff, colored paper, but it is possible to produce a great variety of motions by moving the pieces.

Some string and buttons could be manipulated to produce a variety of actions. All sorts of miscellaneous materials can be used in making animated films.

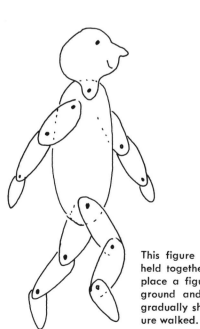

This figure is like a puppet. The joints are held together by brass fasteners. You could place a figure like this on a painted background and get an illusion of motion by gradually shifting the background as the figure walked.

76

The drawings below are based on an animated film that a group of young people made. It describes the antics of a nasty, striped fish that keeps nipping the tails of the other fish. They finally get together and form into one large fish that promptly eats up the striped fish. In the original film, the fish were cut out of paper and painted different colors. The eye of the big fish was made out of two pieces of paper with the pupil a darker color which could be moved about in a very lively fashion.

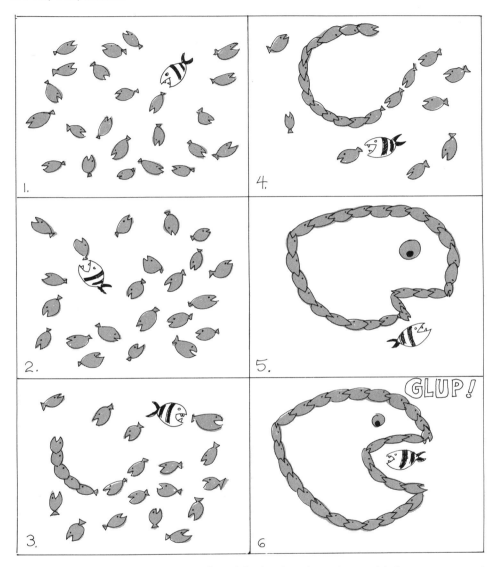

There is still another kind of animation which uses actual objects such as toys, dolls, and clay figures that can be easily shifted about. It is possible to make quite realistic action with this sort of object. The film described on pages 80, 81 was made with only a clay frog, a jointed, stick-it-together plastic toy animal, and a few miscellaneous toys and odds and ends.

How to Do It

Because animated films are made one shot at a time, your camera should have some way of exposing no more than one frame of film at a time. The mechanism that does this is called a *single frame release*. It varies from camera to camera. Sometimes there is a special button you press, sometimes a little adjustment to set. What happens then is that when you press the shutter release, instead of the film running through the camera, there is just a single click, and one frame of film is exposed. You press the trigger again and there is another click and another frame is exposed.

Some cameras—most particularly the less expensive ones—don't have a single frame release. In this case you will have to practice flicking the trigger ever so slightly, so that the camera runs for as brief a time as possible. You may be able to get your camera to expose no more than two or three frames at a time. You may not get quite as smooth results this way, but it is better than nothing.

When you make animated films it is essential that you have your camera fixed in some way to keep it exactly in one place, with absolutely no movement. If the camera moves or shifts—even very slightly—every time you release the shutter, the result will be a jumpy, unpleasant motion on the screen. Therefore, you need a tripod. You must, of course, be very careful not to jostle the tripod. Don't try to get by with your camera propped on a pile of books or held in your hand.

In actual practice it is not necessary to move your subject after each single frame is exposed. You can save yourself a good bit of time by exposing *two* frames, shifting your subject a hair, exposing two more frames, shifting again, and so on.

You'll find that it takes a lot of time to make a short scene that will only last seconds on the screen. The average projector shows about sixteen or eighteen frames a second. That means that five seconds of action on the screen will require that you expose eighty or ninety frames. If you have a long story in mind, plan on spending a good deal of time working on it. You'll see that several hours of work will flash by on the screen in what seems like no time at all.

Questions of exposure, lighting, focus, etc. are the same as in other kinds of filming. If you are working indoors, use artificial-light film. If you are using a Super 8 camera, make sure the filter for use in daylight is pushed out of the way. Focus is particularly important because most animated films are made at quite close range, and even slight focusing errors are quite noticeable. If you are using flood or spotlight, try all kinds of arrangements until you get the kinds of highlights and shadows that you like best.

This is the arrangement that was used to make the animated film described on pages 80, 81. Because the two lights were placed quite close to the action being photographed, very strong lights weren't required. The two bulbs, each 100-watts, provided all the light that was needed.

The illustrations below and opposite describe a short animated film that a friend and I made one rainy Sunday afternoon. The camera was set up as shown, and two plain 100-watt bulbs provided the only lighting. A marine chart was spread over a table—for no reason other than it had a pleasant pattern of shapes, textures, and colors. The blank table top would have been too dark and not very interesting. The table was placed up against a blank white wall. The film used was Kodachrome II, and it was outdoor type. The film should have been indoor type, but I didn't happen to have any, and in fact it didn't make much difference. I didn't particularly care if the frog's color or the dinosaur's complexion was slightly distorted.

1. The film starts as a little toy locomotive comes from the right toward what appears to be a small mountain.

2. The engine circles the mountain, then runs over it.

3. The engine goes off to the right as a stick-figure dinosaur appears.

4. The mountain slowly turns around and we see that it is really a frog. The dinosaur sits down to watch as the frog opens his mouth and a toy airplane comes out.

5. Then a truck comes out, followed by a bird.

6. A pair of scissors comes out.

7. The scissors slowly moves over to the dinosaur and cuts off his head.

8. The frog, evidently a mean character, eats the head.

9. He burps.

10. He brushes his teeth. (During all this action the eyes, which are separate little balls of clay, keep shifting about.)

11. He combs his hair.

12. Still hungry, he eats the brush for dessert.

13. Then he eats his right leg, then his left leg.

14. He turns into a ball and rolls toward the camera. On his back is scratched, *The End.*

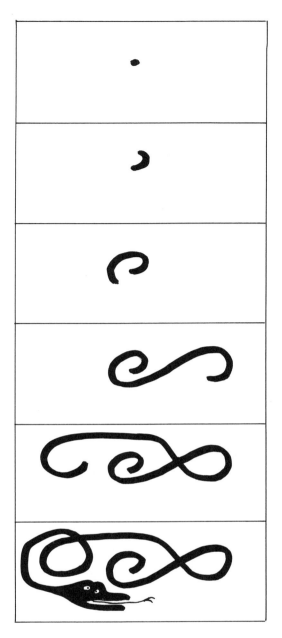

One of the nicest things about animated films is the way you can change the form and meaning of things. A dot can grow into a snake. An airplane can become a tree, a balloon, a house. A pile of blocks can tower higher and higher until blown apart by a flower shot from a cannon. All sorts of wild and fantastic events are possible. The dot turning into a snake is accomplished by simply drawing on a sheet of paper with a heavy, black marking pen. After each exposure the line is extended slightly until the drawing is complete. In the case of the cannon and the building blocks, little squares of paper could be used, and the cannon ball flower could be an actual flower.

Photographs and clippings from books and magazines can be combined and moved about in many ways to produce some strange and amusing animated movies. You'll find this type of film not very different from the making of a collage—only now you can get the parts to move.

There is another kind of filming very similar to animation. It is called time-lapse photography. It is used to show flowers blooming, the sun setting, plants growing, a model being constructed, and anything where there is progressive action. With the camera on a tripod, you expose one frame at a time at pre-determined intervals.

If, for example, a flower took one hour to open, you might make a single frame exposure once every ten seconds. You would end up with a scene lasting about half a minute that would show the flower opening up in an almost magical way.

There are a great many subjects that lend themselves to this sort of examination. How about a fern growing, a bird building a nest, clouds changing shape, the sun setting, ice crystals forming on a window, a room or house being painted, bricks being laid to build a wall, a sand castle eroding?

With both time-lapse and animated films it would be a good idea first to try out a few brief experimental scenes to see how it all works. Then after the tests are processed and you've studied them, you'll be better able to handle something more ambitious.

84

10. Trick Effects

The most obvious trick effects are accomplished by either speeding up or slowing down the camera. If you speed up the camera you get *slow motion*. If you slow down the camera you get *speeded-up* action.

Slow Motion

The normal speed of a movie camera is either sixteen or eighteen frames per second. (The speed varies, depending on the kind of camera.) When the camera speed is increased to thirty-two frames a second, and the film projected at the normal sixteen or eighteen frames, the action will be stretched out. The action that actually took ten seconds will last for twenty seconds on the screen. If you filmed in slow motion someone jumping, and he was off the ground one second, it would appear as if he were up in the air for two seconds when the film was projected.

Many projectors also have variable speed controls. This is another way to speed up or slow down the action.

Slow motion will also help to smooth out pictures taken from a bouncy vehicle. If you take pictures from a car or a train, you will get less jumpy results if you use a slow-motion setting on your camera.

Slow motion is particularly effective when there is some kind of graceful physical movement that you want to emphasize. Dancing, leaping, and sports actions lend themselves to this treatment. It is a way to get lovely, slow, dreamlike movement. You've probably seen countless sports films where the ski jumper or the diver very slowly floats through the air. Or you may have seen scenes of pretty young girls with long blond hair dancing in graceful, flowing motion through sunlit meadows. These effects are all produced by slow motion.

Speeded-up Motion

When the camera is *slowed down* the projected action is speeded up. With the camera set to shoot at eight frames a second, the result is jerky, frantic speed. The effect is usually comical. You may have seen old movies with the Keystone Cops running after someone, in and out of doors, up and down stairs in a ridiculously fast, wild chase. Another classic speeded-up situation is that of a car racing through intersections impossibly fast, narrowly missing trucks and trolleys and scattering pedestrians right and left. This is all filmed with the camera running at less than normal speed.

If, for example, you were making a film and wanted to show your friends rushing to get out of the way of an approaching, unfriendly gorilla, you might well use speeded-up motion. However, as with all tricks, don't use this device too often.

With both slow motion and speeded-up motion, you must adjust your exposure, unless you happen to have the kind of camera that does this automatically. With your camera exposing thirty-two frames a second instead of sixteen or eighteen, less light will be reaching each frame. The picture will be underexposed. You can compensate for less light by changing the lens opening. Set it to the next larger opening. For example, if your normal exposure is f/8 and you change to slow motion, you should change the opening to f/5.6. (Remember, the lower the number, the wider the opening.) With speeded-up motion you do just the opposite.

Another trick effect that is quite simple is to stop the camera in the middle of a scene. Then add, or remove, or change something in the scene—then resume the filming. For example, suppose you had a small can and wanted to "magically" remove many more objects from that can than it could logically hold. In your first shot show one object being taken out of the can. Then stop the camera, place something else in the can. Resume shooting, showing this item being removed, and so on, for as long as you want. In order for this trick to look convincing, the can must remain exactly in place, and the camera must also be firmly secured on a tripod.

You can use this same technique to show somebody in a bathing suit, for example, walking behind a screen, then emerging immediately from the other side of the screen dressed in ski clothes—a magic transformation. Or one person could run behind a tree and somebody else emerge from the other side. There are endless variations on this trick.

If you experiment and try different ways of doing things, you will find all kinds of fascinating possibilities. You might want to experiment with mirrors—shooting half a scene straight, half reflected. There are different kinds of motions that a camera can have. You can walk with it, sit in a swing, or merry-go-round with it. The camera can be tilted, held upside down, jiggled. You can shoot through a pane of colored or textured glass. It is possible to darken a scene by slowly closing your hand over the lens as you are shooting.

It is also possible to experiment with blank film by drawing on it with a felt-tip marker pen, or scratching away the emulsion from black, unexposed lengths of film. You may be surprised at some of the interesting things that can be done this way.

There are many unconventional and experimental ways of using the camera. Keep an eye open for these possibilities. They will add a variety and excitement to most movies.

11. Sound

Sound can add a whole new dimension to movies. It can increase their interest and effectiveness in the most dramatic way. By "sound" we don't mean that the characters in your film will actually be heard talking. The problem of synchronizing lip movement with the actual sounds of the voice is a little beyond the scope of the average filmmaker. But, other than this limitation, anything is possible. You can have music, conversation, poetry, all kinds of background effects, or, in fact, any kind of sound whatsoever. The only piece of equipment you need is a tape recorder. (You can also do a lot with only a phonograph.)

Sound can be more than a mere accompaniment to a film. You might in fact start with a piece of music or sound track and make the film to suit it. In this case you might say the film will accompany the music, rather than the music accompany the film. There was a film made some time ago which was based on the Claude Debussy tone poem, *La Mer* (The Sea). The mood of this music is slow and languid, and does have the feeling of the sea. The film had many scenes of waves, surf breaking (in slow motion), swamplands in fog, fishing boats drifting in calm waters, deserted beaches, swamp reeds, lobster buoys, drifting seaweed, rocks at low tide, and so on. The music and the film fitted together in a most beautiful way, each complementing the other.

You might want to try something like this with a piece of music you find particularly interesting or suggestive. You could use folk music, jazz, rock, an excerpt from a symphony, a sonata, or whatever you think will lend itself to movie treatment.

Music is only one kind of sound you can use with film. If you have a portable tape recorder you can pick up a variety of sounds—most of which can be used with films. For example: sirens, fog horns, footsteps, snoring, water dripping from a faucet (greatly amplified), street noises, racing cars warming up, machinery noises, wind chimes, cheers, children playing, drums or castanets, fingers tapping, a tea kettle hissing, classroom sounds, wood being sawed, popcorn popping, heavy breathing, typewriting, a squeaking rocking chair, and on and on.

Fitting sounds like these to your film can be great fun. Suppose you had a scene of somebody playing the cello, and your sound track was wood being sawed. Or suppose some runners were lined up for the start of a race, and your sound was racing cars warming up. Suppose you photographed a scene of somebody with a bad cold continually wiping his nose, what could be more appropriate than the sound of water slowly plop-plopping from a leaky faucet?

How to Do it

If you want to use nothing more than a single piece of music for your sound, simply choose a record and start your phonograph at the same time you start the projector.

But the problem becomes a little more involved if you want to have two or three different pieces of music or fragments of music during the course of a short film. Here you need a tape recorder and what you have to do is transfer the music from the record to the tape. Do it like this: make a mark on the film where you will start. Do the same with your tape. Now start the phonograph, the tape recorder, (set to "record") and the projector at the same time. (You will need somebody to help you with this.) When you want the music to change, stop all three. Change your record. Then start all three instruments again. You can do this as often as you want.

Instead of playing records into the tape recorder, you could use any other kind of sound—somebody playing the guitar, singing, reciting poetry, beating his chest, chewing gum.

If you own a small, portable cassette recorder, you may have accumulated a variety of interesting sounds that you want to accompany a movie. In this case you will be faced with the problem of editing all these sounds so that they appear in the right order. It is rather difficult to cut apart and edit cassette tapes. So the easiest solution is to borrow another cassette recorder and transfer your various sounds in the order and for the durations you want onto the other recorder. To do this you would follow the procedure outlined above.

Something to bear in mind when you transfer a record onto tape is that you will pick up all kinds of extraneous noises that happen to occur while you are recording if you simply let the phonograph speaker play into the recorder microphone. If somebody coughs, or a door slams, or a fire engine goes by, this will appear on the tape. You can avoid this by getting a set of wires and plugs (called "jacks") so that you can make a direct connection from phonograph to tape recorder. Most recorders and phonographs of good quality have provisions for this kind of hookup.

There may be times, however, when you want "homemade" sounds to appear along with the music. You might be taping some sinister music to accompany a horror movie and decide the effect can be heightened by some thunder, or chains rattling, or mysterious groans and sighs.

There are several other ways to record sound with films. One way is to send the completed film to a processing laboratory where a sound-recording strip (like tape) is added along the edge of the film. Using special equipment, the sound is then recorded onto this strip. You would, of course, have to project this film on a sound projector designed for this kind of film.

Another method uses a cassette recorder that records as the camera shoots. Then it plays back in synchronization with the projector. There are also video tape systems. These use a television camera to record image and sound on tape, rather than on film. The tape can be played back immediately through a sort of television receiver.

But all these methods require rather specialized and expensive equipment and are best left until you've become experienced with the more simple uses of sound, as described here.

12. Making a Movie

The photographs on the following pages are based on a short movie I made recently. Just a few of many scenes are shown here, but they will give you some idea of the story.

This movie is described not because it is any great cinematic work of art—but simply to show you some of the steps, techniques, and thinking that went into the making of a relatively simple film.

The story of *The Orange Box* is simplicity itself. It is about a young fellow who, while walking along the beach one day, finds an orange-colored box. He discovers that anyone who opens it sees all kinds of odd and wonderful visions. Several people try to take the box from him, but in the end. . . .

The title is spelled out with seaweed. My original idea was to scratch the title in the sand. I tried this but the sun was high in the sky and because there were no shadows, the letters didn't show up well. However, I found plenty of seaweed scattered along the high-water line of the beach and this was dark enough to contrast with the sand.

The movie itself starts with a long shot. The camera pans slowly along the horizon and stops at one point where a figure emerges from behind the dunes. By panning the camera, we see a little of the landscape, getting an idea where this action is taking place. It is a kind of orientation and makes a good introduction.

The camera keeps running, following the figure as it climbs over the dunes and makes its way through the grass toward the camera.

Now we have a close-up of our main character. We get a good, first look at John, our hero! The lighting here, which is back lighting, can be a little tricky. The sun is behind the figure shining directly only on shoulders and the back of the neck. Ordinarily the face would be in deep shadow. However, this shot was made where plenty of light was reflected up into the face from the sand. If there was no reflected light, you would have to adjust your exposure for a back lighting situation, or have someone hold a piece of white cardboard to reflect some sunlight up into the shadows.

John jumps off a small sand cliff onto the beach itself. The camera was held at a low angle which makes the leap seem quite dramatic. Slow motion would be useful here. It would make the leap last much longer, and John would almost seem to fly.

Now the camera follows John as he walks along the water's edge. A telephoto setting would be good here because then you could back off with the camera quite a distance and keep the figure in view for a longer time. With a wide angle or normal setting, the figure would seem to approach the camera, pass and then move on at a faster rate of speed than if you were farther away using a telephoto setting. This scene and the preceding one were stretched out for quite a bit of time in order to show some of the beautiful colors of sand and sky and water. If the movie were made elsewhere, other background material or interesting landscape might have been incorporated into the film.

As John walks along the beach he comes across a small orange-colored box, half buried in the sand. He stops, picks it up, turns it over, examining it.

We now move in on the box with a close-up. This would be a good time to use a zoom lens, gradually moving in, getting closer and closer to the box, building suspense. John grabs the lid and opens the box and . . .

. . . all sorts of wild, startling images appear. This part of the movie was great fun to make. I had a number of people put on Halloween masks and jump about in the most frantic way possible. I took very brief shots of each figure. I shot a few frames with my hand held over the lens, resulting in black, unexposed sections. I made a few shots of a piece of blank white cardboard, and then, after the film was processed, I used magic marker pens to color these frames various bright colors. I made some very fast panning shots of sun and trees. And the result was a great jumble of lightning-like images. All of this lasted no more then three or four seconds on the screen. One of these very brief images is of a little boy dancing about waving a fly-swatter. This little fellow, as we learn later, is a "genie" who becomes important at the end of the story. (Actually there were a great many more shots than the four shown on the left.) The purpose of this kaleidoscopic sequence was to suggest that the orange box is really a magic box from which all kinds of wondrous things emerge when the lid is removed.

The kaleidoscopic images stop abruptly as John puts the lid back on the box.

There is a close-up of John's amazed expression. Then he looks about and once again tries opening the box.

Again we have the wild blast of colors and very rapid, confused images as before. Yes, this is definitely a magic box!

John puts the lid back on the box and runs off along the beach.

He passes two people who are sitting on the beach. They look up as he passes, see the box and decide they want it. In this shot, the camera has been following John. But the camera stops panning as John passes the two figures. It remains on them as they look at one another, then get up and follow after John.

Now we have some chase scenes. This is the kind of action many movie-makers love. It is always dramatic and provides an opportunity to include a lot of violent movement in different settings.

There is a variety of scenes at this point in the movie which try to build up the tension of the chase. In one shot, I held the camera and ran along, slightly in front of the pursuers, getting a close-up of their faces. The result was a very jumpy and unsteady picture, but it captured the spirit of the chase.

As the chase continues, the background changes as the action shifts to different areas and different parts of the beach. This shot is a sort of dolly shot made from a moving car. I shot out of the car window while a friend drove along slowly, keeping pace with the running figure. This was a different kind of shot from the previous ones and lent a little visual variety to the chase.

Finally, John is cornered. The two chasers manage to get him up against the wall of a shed on an old pier. They start to close in on him.

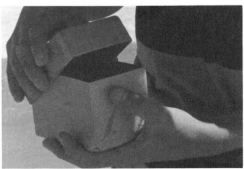

But at the last minute, John opens the orange box.

There is another burst of blurred motion, color, brief fragmented actions—and then the little genie appears.

It turns out that the genie has a magic fly swatter. He swats the two "bad guys" on the head with it and they immediately fall to the ground. Our hero is saved!

John puts the cover back on the box. But the genie remains and the two of them skip off. The two bodies lie sprawled out on the pier. The camera was held at a low angle so that the bodies would remain in view as John and the genie disappear down the end of the dock.

The last shot is "The End" chalked on a piece of old board.

The methods and procedures that I used to make this movie are not the only correct or proper ones. If you were making it, you would most certainly do it in an altogether different way—your way. But this account will give you some idea of what is involved in making a film, so that when you set out to do one of your own you will have some notion of what you will encounter.

Now that you've read this book and know something about how movies are made, I hope you'll go out and, with imagination, humor, and courage, make all kinds of interesting films of your own.